Matthew Clark

BASKETBALL

FOR

KIDS

A Complete Illustrated Guide for Kids and Beginners Players!

Basics, Skills, Game Rules, Glossary

TABLE OF CONTENT

INTRODUCTION 5

BASIC RULES FOR PLAYING BASKETBALL 10

OUT OF BOUNDS 13

SHOOT THE BALL THROUGH THE HOOPS AND SCORE POINTS. 15

DRIBBLING 17

PASSING 35

SHOOTING 38

REBOUNDING 42

OFFENSIVE DRILLS 43

DEFENSIVE DRILLS 44

VIOLATIONS 47

FOULS 51

PLAYER POSITIONS 58

GAME CLOCK 64

HEALTH BENEFITS OF PLAYING BASKETBALL 66

EATING RIGHT 83

INTRODUCTION

- Basketball games are an exciting sport. It's fun, fun, and children learn valuable lessons that can apply to other aspects of life. The good news for parents who want their children to take part in this sporting activity is that basketball can introduce at a very young age.

- primary motor and coordination skills such as ball dribbling and shooting can introduce when the child is two years old.

- The youth league accepts children aged 5 or 6. This is an excellent opportunity for children to learn the basics of gaming. You can introduce concepts such as the hustle and bustle, teamwork, athleticism and attitude as well as more technical aspects of the game such as footwork, defence, and shooting mechanics.

- Participation in youth sports like basketball brings many potential benefits to children and teenagers. They are Participating in youth sports as a means of promoting relationships, peer appreciation and leadership skills. It can also lay the foundation for an active and healthy lifestyle for adults. Basketball has one of the highest participation rates in youth sports, which makes it an excellent opportunity for young athletes to take advantage of these benefits. However, overemphasis on young people's success in sports can prevent children from realizing the benefits of participating and ultimately limiting their skills.

- Participation in sport offers children and adolescents short-term and long-term physical and psychosocial benefits. However, overemphasizing the competitive success of youth sports can limit the benefits of participation and increase the risk of injury, burnout and withdrawal from physical activity. The American Basketball Association and the American Basketball Association have recently assembled a group of leading experts to share their applied research and practice to address these issues. The review includes a group analysis of many of existing studies on youth participation in sport and the related health, performance and psychosocial results. On this basis, we will provide age-specific recommendations for participating in basketball to promote a healthy and positive experience for youth basketball players.

BASIC RULES FOR PLAYING BASKETBALL

- Basketball is a team sport.

- Two teams of five players each try to score by firing the ball in a hoop 10 feet above the ground.

- The game is played on a rectangular floor called a playing field with circles on both ends.

- The court is divided into two main sections by the centerline of the court.

- If the attacking team puts the ball behind the centerline, it takes 10 seconds for the shot to cross the centerline.
- If not, the defence wins the ball.
- If the attacking team places the ball over the centerline, it cannot hold the ball in the area behind the centerline.
- If so, the defence receives the ball.
- The ball moves in the direction of the basket or dribbles in the course of the playing field. The team with the ball is called a crime. The team without the ball is called defence.
- The defence tries to steal the ball to fight shots, to deflect the pass and to rebound.

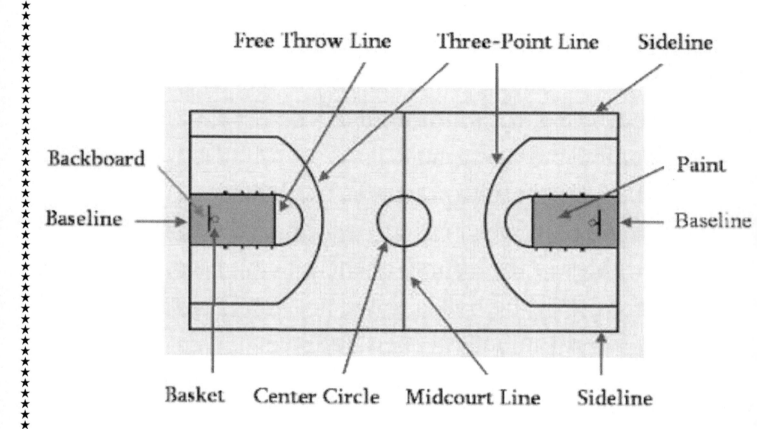

Free Throw Line   Three-Point Line   Sideline

Backboard

Baseline   Paint

Baseline

Basket   Center Circle   Midcourt Line   Sideline

OUT OF BOUNDS

- All basketball courts played in huge rectangles.

  You or the ball must not touch the outside of the rectangular line.

  This term is said not to apply.

  The ball is thrown out of range but cannot return once it is in play. If you do not have the ball, you can cross the line without penalty.

SHOOT THE BALL THROUGH THE HOOPS AND SCORE POINTS.

- In basketball, an attacking player can earn 1-3 points for a shot, depending on where the shot was fired on the ground.
  In most places, a semicircle of about 6.1 m (20 feet) extends from the tire at the "three-point line", from which the shot is worth the extra points. Within this bow, each shot is worth two points.Each foul shot is worth one point and is taken from the free-throw line, 4.6 m from the tire. If a foul occurs during a shooting attempt or if another team collects too many fouls, the player receives 1 to 3 free throws. You get a

foul if another team hits your body when you take a shot. If you make a shot, you will receive points and a free throw. If you make a mistake, you will receive two free throws.

DRIBBLING

You must dribble to move the ball. Dribbling is a term used to bounce and walk with the ball without picking it up or using both hands. If you use both sides or pick them up and dribble again, they are called double dribbles and the opposing team wins the ball. If you keep your hands on the ball, dribbling improves.

Dribble - It is essential to break into the tire, move the ball across the field, get out of the defence and find the right fast lane. There are different types of dribbling.

• PACE CHANGE

It is relatively easy for a defending player to protect you using dribble to keep the ball moving at a constant speed. He /she just matches your gear and is with you. It complicates the work of a defender. Please change the pace.

To change the pace, you need to change the speed at which the ball moves forward. Once the defender matches your speed, slow down the ride. As soon as he /she slows down, he accelerates faster.

Tempo dribbling like stop-and-go (see my tip, stop-and-go dribbling) is a great way to deal with defenders who defend you firmly and positively.

20

• CROSSOVER DRIBBLING

Crossover dribbling is one of the most effective ways to keep control of the ball against intense pressure. It is the primary tool that point guards use when climbing coats under defensive pressure. But it's also a great way to free yourself up for scoring chances. You can use it to reach the basket and make room between you and your defender. Crossover dribble helps set up jump shots (move later).

• **HOW TO MAKE A CROSSOVER:**

Start at one end of the square. Place the ball in your right hand (right or left-handed are not crucial as this drill requires both sides to perform this action with the same effect).

Use your right foot to move the ball from right to left in one drop. If you did it right, your left foot should hit the ground as if the ball had reached you. Start with the ball in your left hand and repeat this movement.

Do this exercise at walking pace until you can rely on both your footwork and control of the ball until you can do this while moving at your walking pace. Ideally, you can do this with a full sprint after a few weeks on the floor above and below. This exercise should be for 10 minutes, and the player rests at one- minute intervals for 30 seconds.

• BEHIND THE BACK

One step to consider when playing basketball is to put it on your back.
If you put a basketball in the back, you can get a high percentage of shots and get precise passes. The basketball behind the retreat is useful if the defender blocks you and is too close to cross it. A movement is when you want to change the direct path because the first drive has disconnected. Placing a basketball behind your back is safer than a crossover and faster than a spinning motion. So, it's between the two movements. There are several things behind a back move that you can do. Both should be added to the game and applied to the most comfortable situation. The

difference is in footwork and where the ball bounces before hitting your hand.

The first way to do back-to-back movement is to put the ball behind your back, take your feet off your shoulders, and land with both feet at the same time. In this case, the ball should jump directly behind your back and cross and land on your other hand. This method is a little slower than the second, but easier to do because you can use basketball to get more control over your body position.

The second way to make this move is faster than the first, but is more difficult at game speed and may require more practice to reduce the likelihood of forced sales. This style is about moving the attack towards the edge or wherever you need to move it and wrapping the ball around your body as soon the defender cuts you out. The reason why this is faster and more difficult is that, unlike the first two-foot stop, it doesn't interrupt your running step.

Not only that, but the ball also doesn't bounce back like the first ball. The ball will jump on your right. For example, if you run to the left and a defender cuts you, take the shot, wrap it around your back before contacting it, and the ball is next to your right hip or right foot. You want to bounce off the floor, with the right hand.

However, if the ball hits the other hand, the ball may be exposed. In this case, the defender can deflect the ball. To prevent this, turn in the direction you want to go to the defender and make sure you are lower than the defender. Daniel Washington is an expert in athletic performance and the basics of basketball. If you want to learn more about playing basketball, be sure to read the other articles. Thank you for reading this article about dribbling back.

- **DRIBBLE THE PULL BACK**

  - The player starts with the ball over the key and a dummy defender.

  - When the drill starts, the player drives hard to the right elbow.

  - When you reach the angle, use the pull back dribble to return to the top of the key and attack the block on the left.

  - Pull the dribble from the left elbow back onto the top of the key.

• At the top of the button, make another move and attack the right angle to get a pull-up jump shot.

• This concludes an iteration.

• The next player in the row can move, or the player can reset and then move left.

- **LESS DRIBBLING**

As the name suggests, slight dribbling means that the ball bounces and is closest to the ground. It effectively secures the ball from the guard. It requires dribbling to reach and limit the space your opponents can enter.

- **SPEED DRIBBLING**

When you have the ball in the open, you need to use your time to control the ball and your body. In general, you should use speed dribbling to achieve your goals. Speed dribbling used when the player is not firmly protected and forced to defend the ball excessively. It gives him /her an excellent opportunity to dribble faster and reach a certain distance.

- **BASIC DRIBBLING**

This type of dribbling occurs by slowing movements that believed to stop. It makes the opponent think that you finish passing the ball. However, as soon you get a response from your opponent, you have to explode quickly and run through your opponent.

- **DRIBBLE HOCKEY**

It uses a fake head and shoulders combination with sudden changes in pace. It applies to distract the defender from the corner.

- **DRIBBLING BACKWARD**

  If you are well protected, you can use reverse
  dribbling to prevent your opponent from stealing
  the ball.
  The main disadvantage of this dribbling is that it
  tends to lose sight of the ball for some time,
  which causes it to catch the shot from the back.

- **HALF DRIBBLE BACKWARD**

  It is close to reverse dribbling.
  In this case, however, the player must turn 90
  degrees from their original position. In this case,
  the movement must be very fast so that the
  opposing team's player cannot catch the ball.

PASSING

- Good attack requires a good pass from the player. It will help you find open men, find great shooters, and stay away from defenders. There are different types of trails that you need to learn.

  - <u>Overhead</u>

  - <u>Chest pass</u>

  - <u>Bounce pass</u>

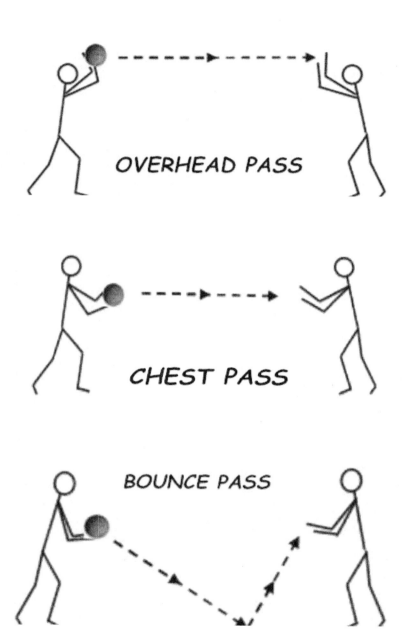

OVERHEAD PASS

CHEST PASS

BOUNCE PASS

- It is the most critical part. You must pass the ball on to your colleague. As a learner, you need to know how to go the right way as the game progresses. You need to practice some breast passes with other trainees. Overhead passes are also allowed in this sport. It is, therefore, vital to learning how to use overhead paths. The ball should be held directly above your head. Bounce passes are also crucial in basketball. If you pass the ball on here, you and your teammates will aim for the third quarter.

SHOOTING

- The ball must go through the basket to score. There are three places where a person can shoot. Earn 3 points by standing behind the 3-point line, a large arch around the basket, and placing it in the basket.

  All other places in front of the sheet are worth 2 points. The third place is from the free-throw line. If you are fouled and throw free throws, each free throw is worth 1 point.

  Shoot - The goal of the game is to win and win the most points.

  Therefore, it is essential to improve team shooting to win the game.

<u>There are several ways to get a match:</u>

- Jump shot
- Dunk
- Alley hut
- Free throw
- Hang up
- 3-point shot
- Hook shot
- You need to know how to shoot to collect points at this port. All beginners must learn this skill and different shooting techniques.
- There are box drills and ball drills.
- Several players, each with one ball, are required for a ball drill. They all end up in an uncomfortable position, dropping their elbows,

jumping, and shooting from the highest point.

• Box drills are performed with a single ball, with players on the right and left sides of the field. The player on the right takes a jump shot in the back yard, and the player on the left runs up and receives the rebound from making his shot. The ball moves from the player on the right to another player while maintaining the continuity of the drill.

REBOUNDING

- Rebound indispensable to regain possession or to regain possession after a shot. In general, the team with the most rebounds after the game has more chances to collect points.

OFFENSIVE DRILLS

- Attack - This is the only chance that the team will get a shot in the basket and score. A correct attack requires coordination between players and individual skills to play a decent game. It is a fight in which the players are lined up separately under each basket. The next player is ready to grab the rebound and repeat the exercise so that the first player on another side dribbles into another basket with full speed.

DEFENSIVE DRILLS

- Defend - To have a chance to score and win, the team must take appropriate defenses and stop hitting the opponent. As I said: "Good defense is a good attack."
If you practice this, two players must stand between the balls. One is defensive, and the other is aggressive. After the signal, the defending player uses his position to prevent other players from getting the ball.

- **MOVE**

  There are several types of basketball moves that are important for performing both good attacks and good defense. Movement can help you find open men, take good shots, and play great.

- **STOP DRIBBLING**

If you dribble the ball, you have decided to pick it up; you are only allowed one step. The foot you don't want to step on must remain on the floor. Moving the other leg is considered movement and is illegal. As you walk, other teams win the ball. After picking up the ball, the only way is to pass the ball around or swing it. A prop can rotate and rotate around a planted foot, but it cannot slide or leave the ground.

VIOLATIONS

Knowing the types of basketball injuries will improve the game:

- **Walking/traveling** I run more than "a step and a half" without dribbling the ball. When you have stopped dribbling move the swivel base.

- **Wear/palm**. When the player dribbles the ball sideways or sometimes too far under the ball.

- **Double dribble**. Dribbling the ball with both hands at the same time or picking up the dribbling and then dribbling is a double dribble.

47

- **Hero Ball**. Sometimes two or more opponents hold the ball at the same time. To avoid long and or violent fights, the referee stops the action and passes the ball on to the spinning base to one or the other team.

- **Goalkeeper**. If a defending player interferes with a shot on a basket, on the backboard after touching the backboard or in the cylinder over the edge, chance counted goal posture. It is an injury if an aggressive player commits it and the ball passed to the opposing team for a throw-in.

- **Black coat injury**. After the offence has brought the ball over the centerline, it cannot cross the line while holding the ball. In this case, the ball is passed on to the other team to overtake the incoming pass.

- **Time limit.** Players who pass the ball on within 5 seconds. Otherwise, the ball will give to another team. Other time limits include the rule that the player must not hold the ball for more than 5 seconds. There are also time limits for shots in some states and levels where a team must try a chance in a specific time.

Traveling

Illegal dribble

Palming/ carrying the ball

Over and back

3-second violation

* Open hand - run end line

5-second violation

10-second violation

Free throw, designated spot. or other violation

Excessively swinging arm(s)/elbow(s)

Kicking

FOULS

A foul occurs when a person touches the ball. If you protect someone with the ball, you cannot feel or hit them. Fraud can also be committed by outside the ball. Standing -out, beating and stumbling are all criminal offences. These are not allowed in basketball.

Foul-In many cases the defender accidentally touches the opponent/ or the ball handler moves aggressively towards the defender. However, fouls also used as a strategy to stop the clock and prevent shooting players from quickly scoring. Learning how to deal with fouls is vital in the game.

Personal fouls:

Personal fouls include any type of illegal physical contact.

- Beat

- Press

- blow

- Hold

- Illegal selection /screen - when an aggressive player is on the move. An offensive player stretches his limbs and makes physical contact with the defender to block the defender's pass.

➤ **Personal foul penalties:** If the player shoots during the foul, he receives two free throws if he misses a shot, but only one if he misses a chance. If a player dirty and miss an opportunity during a three-point goal, you will receive three free throws. If a foul occurs when shooting a 3-point shot, the player gets 1 free throw. Therefore, he was able to score 4 points in the game.

➤ **Incoming**. If you lazy while not shooting, the ball will be given to the team that fouled it. You leave the ball on the next side or baseline and pass the ball on to the field within 5 seconds.

➢**One and one**. If the fouled team has more than seven fouls in play, the fouled player receives a free throw. With his first shot, he gets another free throw.

➢**10 or more fouls**. If the fouled team has ten or more fouls, the fouled player receives two free throws.

➢**Charge**. An attack foul committed when a player pushes or destroys a defensive player. The ball awarded to the team in which the foul committed.

➢**To block.** A block is an illegal personal contact that occurs because the defender does not set up a position in time to prevent an enemy from falling into the basket.

➢**Malicious foul**. Violent contact with the enemy. It includes hitting, kicking and hitting.

➢**Intentional foul.** When a player physically contacts another player with no reasonable effort to steal the ball. It is a call for a judicial decision.

➤ **Technical foul.** Technical foul. Players or coaches can commit this type of foul. It does not include the player contact or the ball, but the "type" of the game. Poor wording, obscene expression, obscene gestures or even controversy can see, as technical foul, as can technically details on improperly filling out the scorebook or warming up dunks. I'm going

Illegal use of hand

Hand check

Holding

Blocking

Pushing or charging

Player-control foul

Team-control foul

Intentional foul

Double foul

Technical foul

PLAYER POSITIONS

• **MIDDLE**. The Centre is usually the most significant player. They typically placed near the basket.

• **AGGRESSIVE** - The goal of the Centre is to open the way and shoot. It is also your responsibility to block the defenders, known as picking or screening, and to free other players to drive to the goal in the basket. The Centre expected to get some aggressive rebounds and bring them back.

• Defense In defence, the Centre's primary responsibility is to block shots and passes in critical areas to prevent enemies from shooting. They also expected to get a lot of rebounds because they are more prominent.

• **TRANSFER**. Your next higher player is probably your striker. Strikers may need to play under the tires, but they can also use in the wings and corners.

• **AGGRESSIVE** - It is the striker's responsibility to release the pass, shoot outside, hit the gate, and bounce off.

• Defensive tasks include preventing and rebounding the drive to the goal.

• **GUARD.** These may be your shortest players, and

they should be good at dribbling, seeing, and fitting the field quickly. Your task is to put the ball on the court and trigger an aggressive game.

• **DRIBBLING**, passing and set up on the offensive are the primary responsibility of the guardian. You must also be able to drive to the basket and shoot from the area.

• Defense In defence, the guards, are responsible for stealing paths to compete for shots, preventing driving to the tires and boxing.

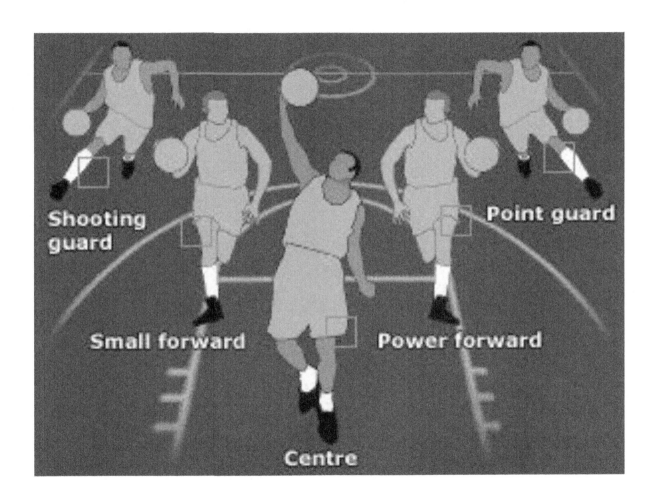

POINTS

If a team makes a basket, they get 2 points, and the ball goes to the other side.

• If a basket or field goal created outside the 3-point arc, the basket is worth 3 points. Free throws are worth 1 point.

• Free throws given to teams in a variety of formats, including the number of halved fouls and or the type of foul committed.

• If you dirty the shooter, the shooter will always receive two or three free throws, depending on where you shoot. If he crosses the 3-point line, he gains three shots.

• Other types of fouls will not receive free throws until a certain number has accumulated for half (referred to as "team foul").

• If this number reached, the fouled player given the option "1 and 1". If he makes the first free throw, he will try the second time. If he misses the first shot, the ball is thrown back and lives.

GAME CLOCK

Each game is divided into sections and each level has two halves.

• At the university, each half lasts 20 minutes.

• Below the high school, half is divided into quarters of eight minutes (sometimes six minutes). For professionals, a quarter takes 12 minutes.

• There is a gap of a few minutes between the halves. The quarterly difference is relatively short.

• If the scores at the end of the regulation are the same, there will be overtime of different lengths until a winner appear.

HEALTH BENEFITS OF PLAYING BASKETBALL

It's no secret that an active child is more likely to become a productive adult.

Children today have many options about which sport they want to play.

The federal government has partnered with 30 national sports organizations, including Basketball Queensland, to set up a sports school, a program designed to encourage children's interest and participation in sport from an early age.

• HOW BASKETBALL BENEFITS YOUR CHILD

Useful for building muscle during whole-body training.

Basketball is a high-intensity sport that offers full-body workouts, including hand-eye coordination skills such as running, jumping, dribbling and passing the ball, shooting, and more. Keeping the game moving can also help promote endurance and muscle building. This type of exercise also helps to increase aerobic capacity, energy levels and metabolism, which leads to increased concentration at school.

• THE IMPORTANCE OF FUNCTIONAL SPORTINESS

It is an important skill both on and off the field. The Aussie Hoops program focuses on allowing everyone the opportunity to participate in a fun and non-competitive environment. Players hold hands with their opponents and referees every time they play and to take responsibility for their performance rather than blaming others for things.

• IMPROVE SOCIAL DEVELOPMENT AND TEAMWORK

Playing team sports like basketball is a great opportunity for children to build lasting friendships with their teammates and to be surrounded, by coaches and older players who serve as role models for young players. Participation in team sports also underscores the importance of working as a team to achieve and collaborate on sporting goals. Basketball teaches children how vital communication skills are, how important it is to listen to each other, and how effective teamwork is

• THE IMPORTANCE OF RESPECTING AUTHORITY

Sport is a great way to discipline your children by following the rules of the game and being led by coaches, officials and team members. The Aussie Hoops program allows children the opportunity to interact regularly with coaches, referees and other players to understand the importance of listening to and respecting others on and off the pitch. Will help.

• IMPROVE SELF-ESTEEM

Participation in sport is ideal for characterizing a child and can contribute significantly to self-esteem. The Aussie Hoops program emphasizes the fun and joy of basketball, rather than differentiating children's self-esteem by winning, losing or scoring. When a child notices an improvement in skill levels and development, they become more confident in their court skills. Being in a collaborative team environment with coaches, teammates and encouraging friends and family is invaluable to contribute to the growth.

• CARDIOVASCULAR HEALTH

That is a big problem. If cardiovascular health is the only benefit of playing basketball, it's worth it. Cardiovascular health is the health of the heart and blood vessels and is vital for the prevention of strokes, heart attacks and other heart diseases.

The different movements, stops and starts, as well as the various activities in basketball, are very similar to circuit training, which is known to be very good for cardiovascular health. Often referred to as "cardio" training, it increases your heart rate and pumps blood through your veins.

• CALORIES BURNED

Having safe and efficient methods of burning calories is a massive benefit to your health. To lose weight or maintain a healthy weight, you need to burn calories. It is related to cardiovascular health and helps prevent diabetes and other weight-related problems. Unlike some gimmicks, medications, or surgeries, basketball is a very safe and natural way to burn calories. As mentioned above, the aerobic exercise provided by basketball burns calories efficiently and safely.

• OFFERS STRENGTH TRAINING

Weight training is an integral part of physical health, but it doesn't necessarily mean that it must look like Arnold Schwarzenegger. The real goal is to maintain enough muscle condition to perform daily activities relatively quickly. Of course, there is nothing wrong with building more muscle and strength if you want to, but when it comes to basic strength training, basketball can do it quickly.

• BUILD UP THE BONE STRENGHT

Without proper movement, your body's bones begin to deteriorate. It eventually becomes weaker, weaker, and makes your bones more comfortable to break. Bone strength is an integral part of your physical health. Basketball helps us build bone strength through everything we've mentioned above. Aerobic and strength training that works on many muscles in the body to strengthen the bones. As with muscles, the more you use it, the stronger it gets.

• STRENGTHENS THE IMMUNE SYSTEM

The immune system is an integral part of your health because it protects you from illness. The healthier you are, the better your immune system is because it is closely related to your overall health.

Basketball strengthens the immune system by improving overall health. Heavy basketball also causes sweating, which removes unwanted toxins from your body and strengthens your immune system.

• COORDINATION AND MOTOR SKILLS

These skills affect almost everything in everyday life. Walking, sitting, driving, or any other physical activity. If you are not balanced, you can fall easily and injure yourself with simple daily tasks.

Your coordination and athletic performance refined when playing basketball. Almost everything you do in basketball, including running, panning, dribbling, passing, shooting, and bouncing, is improved with these skills.

• SPACE AND BODY AWARENESS

These types of things are consistent with coordination and motor skills, but the ability to see where you compared to other objects around you. It helps you assess the perception of distance and depth.

Basketball is ideal for spatial recognition. You have to determine the length to your shopping cart and how difficult it is. You have to learn how close you are to other players. Basketball trains your muscles and brain so that you can react appropriately depending on the distance and the space around you.

• STRESS RELIEF

Stress can affect our body's health in many ways. Blood pressure, heart health and the immune system are just a few of the things we can sacrifice when we are under stress.
Even when you are on the court playing, basketball can significantly reduce weight. The fun of playing and the release of energy are beneficial to reduce the burden of your life.

• IMPULSIVE DECISION MAKING AND QUICK THINKING

Basketball is not only a quick game that requires a lot of physical skill but also a mind game that you have to think. This sport requires concentration so that you can deal with what is happening on the court accurately and quickly and make the right decisions to guide the ball. You also need to assess the environment of the courts around you and make an instant decision based on the actions of other players on the court.

• Hand and eye coordination skills
Basketball requires a lot of hands and eye
coordination as well as whole-body
coordination. Practice or play basketball,
whether it's a pass or a shot. Develop these
skills as you navigate the rebounds, dribbles,
and squares on the next turn.

• SHAPE

Playing basketball also helps burn calories. With a quick sideways movement, running and jumping enable aerobic exercise, and a person weighing 165 pounds can consume about 600 calories. A person who weighs 250 pounds can waste about 900 calories. It shows that it is also very active as an entertaining fitness routine. As a result, you may not feel like targeting the gym to burn calories.

EATING RIGHT

Basketball is an intermittent and intense sport that requires both physical agility and mental strength. The energy requirement during the basketball season is very high and can be even higher during training outside the season.

Choosing foods that provide energy to support competition and training is essential and can be very difficult. Unlike high-level college and professional basketball players who have the resources and the ability to eat correctly, college players and high school athletes can access resources in a variety of ways.

• DAILY ENERGY REQUIREMENTS

The energy needs for high school basketball players can be significant. In a recent study by Silva et al. The study conducted measured the energy consumption of female and male high school basketball players during the season at over 3,500 and 4,600 kcal /day, respectively. Total energy intake is vital to counteract weight loss during the season, but the calorie source is to provide the muscles with the right kind of fuel.

• CARBOHYDRATES

Carbohydrates are the fuel that muscles prefer during strenuous exercises like basketball. The body stores carbohydrates as glycogen in the liver and skeletal muscle. Glucose stored in the liver maintain blood sugar levels during meals. THE liver stores 75-100 g of carbs, enough to keep blood sugar during a 12-hour fast. Most people consume a lot of their liver glycogen before they wake up in the morning. Therefore, athletes need to eat before the morning workout. -Another 300-400 g of carbohydrates stored in the skeletal muscle. Unlike liver glycogen, muscles use a carbohydrate supply to promote exercise, and exercise can almost double the amount of glycogen that a muscle can store. And run. When muscle glycogen stores are full, most athletes are enough to recharge high-intensity activities for 90 to 100 minutes. Terms such as "crash against the wall" and "bondage" used to describe what happens when an athlete lacks glycogen storage. Individual exercises and games may not be enough to reduce muscle glycogen, but insufficient carbohydrate intake in combination with daily use can reduce muscle glycogen for several days. It can cause the player to get tired or feel a "heavy leg".

Basketball players should follow a high-carb diet. At least 55% of the total calories in the diet should come from foods rich in carbohydrates such as fruits, vegetables, bread, pasta and rice. Most sports nutritionists recommend weight-dependent carbohydrate intake to ensure that athletes can consume enough energy from their carbohydrates. The recommended range for carbohydrate intake for basketball players is 5-7 (and up to 10) g / kg body weight (see example diet below). The amount depends on the time played and the season (pre-season, postseason, postseason).

• PROTEIN

Protein is vital for gaining and maintaining lean body mass. Many athletes take supplements and strive to increase dietary protein to increase muscle mass. However, if you eat a balanced diet all day long and consume enough energy and protein, it may not usually be needed. Studies show that a protein intake of 1.8 g / kg body weight is the upper limit for muscle protein synthesis. For a 263 kg player, this is about 115 g of protein. A player weighing 180 kg (82 kg) may need up to 150 g. As shown in the example menu, this can quickly fill with sufficient energy consumption. Eating more than this amount of protein is not harmful to a healthy person, but often replaces the energy from carbohydrates in the diet. It is the preferred fuel for muscles, as mentioned above. When the muscles are low in carbohydrates, they use proteins, inefficient metabolic processes that give athletes a feeling of fatigue and exhaustion. The recommended daily protein intake for basketball players is 1.4-1.7 g / kg body weight.

- **THICK**

Dietary fat is essential for hormone and cell membrane synthesis and proper immune function. Athletes strive for heart-healthy fats such as monounsaturated fats (olive oil, avocado) and omega-3 fats (salmon, linseed), saturated fats (beef fat, lard) and trans fats (margarine). And processed oils) foods that should avoid).

• PRE-GAME MEAL

The goal of the pre-competition diet is to eliminate the distraction of hunger and reduce the risk of gastrointestinal problems while meeting the body's energy needs (e.g. replacing liver glycogen). A proper diet or diet should be high in carbohydrates, low in fat and low in fibre (see Table 1). A good guideline for carbohydrates is the following equation:

(Kg body weight) x (time before the competition) = grams of carbohydrates
For example, a player who weighs 68 kg and eating 3 hours before the game could eat 68 Kilograms of x 3 hours = 204 grams of

carbohydrates. It is equivalent to a small meal that includes turkey bread and 1 -ounce pretzel. Cereal bars and 1 l (33 oz) Gatorade Thirst Quencher. If this player had a meal an hour before the game, only about 70 grams of carbohydrates would consume. A tasty snack is 1 litre

of Gatorade Thirst Quencher and 1 ounce of a pretzel. Every player must find the best food and drink for them by experimenting before and during training. Everyone is a little different, and a player's "happy" meal can make her teammates have stomach cramps.

- **FUEL IN THE GAME**

A basketball game lasts 32 to 48 minutes, depending on the level. Players are less likely to drain muscle and liver glycogen stores, but carbohydrate supplementation during play helps maintain fourth-quarter performance. Studies have shown that supplementing subjects with carbohydrates instead of placebo supports both cognitive function five and sprint speed 1 in basketball protocols. Again, players have to experiment during training to find the best food and drink for them. However, many uses Gatorade Thirst Quencher, sports gels or chewing items, parts of sports bars or oranges. The recommended amount of carbohydrates consumed to maintain performance is 30-60 g / h. Given the length of the game, athletes must, therefore, find the best solution to get 30-60 g of carbohydrates during the game. For example, Gatorade Thirst Quencher can meet your carbohydrate needs in 16-32 ounces and provide liquids and electrolytes.

Dehydration must affect basketball performance. Therefore, all forms of carbohydrate supplementation should include hydration. Fortunately, basketball is suitable for natural interruptions to the action. Time-outs, quarterly breaks and half-time breaks offer players the opportunity to refuel and hydrate themselves. As mentioned above, eating food and liquids during exercise should be practiced to determine the most effective strategy. To establish a person's sweat rate, wipe off the excess sweat and weigh the player in the same clothes before and after a lesson. When they lost weight, they did not drink enough fluids and had to consume an additional 16 ounces per pound of weight loss on their next exercise. Each player should try to weigh less than 2% during training and games (e.g. £ 3 for a £ 150 player). The amount each player needs to maintain hydration varies. Likewise, every player can like and tolerate different forms of carbohydrates. Players should be encouraged to find the best combination of food and hydration to reduce the risk of stomach cramps while maintaining hydration and energy.

GLOSSARY

A

Alley-Oop: one player jumps and catches a pass from another player and simultaneously dunks the ball or shoots it in before landing

Assist: statistic that occurs when a player passes the ball to someone who scores after receiving the pass.

B

Backboard: rectangular piece of wood or fiberglass the rim is attached to

Box Out: a shot goes up, players use this technique, which involves widening their stance and arms and using their body as a barrier to get in better rebounding position

C

<u>Carry</u>: penalty, occurs when a player holds the ball excessively at the apex while dribbling

<u>Charge</u>: penalty, occurs when an offensive player with the ball runs into a stationary defensive player and knocks him or her over

D

<u>Double Dribble</u>: penalty occurs when a player dribbles the ball with both hands

E

Elbow: area of the court where the free throw line meets the side of the key or paint

F

Fast Break: offensive action where a team attempts to advance the ball and score as quickly as possible after a steal, blocked shot or rebound

K

Key: painted area that makes up the free throw lane. Also referred to as the paint

L

Lay-Up: shot taken close to the hoop, usually when a player is moving toward the basket

M

Man-to-Man: defensive strategy in which each player on the defensive team guards one person on the opposing team

O

Outlet: offensive strategy in which a player who gathers a defensive rebound passes to a teammate in an attempt to quickly begin the next possession

P

Press: defensive strategy where the defenders guard the opposing team the full length of the court instead of waiting on the opposite side for the offense to come across

Post Up: offensive strategy in which a player gets the ball in the post area with his or her back to the basket

R

<u>Rebound</u>: a player from either team retrieves the ball and gains possession after a missed shot

S

<u>Screen</u>: offensive strategy in which a player without the ball stands in the way of a defensive player. The offensive player must remain stationary during the process, or a moving screen will be called and the result will be an offensive foul and a turnover

<u>Swish</u>: made basket where the ball avoids the rim and touches nothing but the net, creating a "swish" sound

T

Travel: penalty, which results in a turnover, where an offensive player moves his or her pivot foot illegally or takes three steps without dribbling the ball

Turnover: the offensive team loses possession of the ball by way of an offensive foul, steal or out-of-bounds violation

Z

Zone Defense: defensive strategy in which players guard a specific zone or area of the court instead of a specific player on the opposing te

Kind reader,

Thank you very much. I hope you enjoyed the book.

Can I ask you a big favor?

I would be grateful if you would please take a few minutes to leave me a gold star on Amazon.

Thank you again for your support.

Matthew Clark

Printed in Great Britain
by Amazon